PROLOGUE

Everyone has a story, and everyone is fighting their own battles. This is a story of a girl who seemed to have a "perfect" life, a girl who did well in school and had friends. This is a story of that same girl and her stay in a mental hospital. This is the story of a girl who battled with anxiety, depression, self-harm, and suicidal thoughts. This is the story of a girl who looked fine, but wasn't really. This is the story of a girl who was sick and dying inside, yet still smiling on the outside. I am that girl, and this is my story.

Journey (Written June 5th, 2013)

all I seem to be able to write is poetry these days
my words show themselves in the forms of sadness and despair
they envelope the reader like their favourite blanket
the one they curl up with in their comfiest chair

I wish that I could write about happy things like sunshine and rainbows
but that is not the way I feel, I feel depressed and filled with sorrow
the things I write about are not pleasant for some;
suicide, self harm, and mental illnesses

this is my reality right now and I'm inviting the reader to join me
on my confusing journey, trying to figure out the intricacies of my brain
although I warn you, do not stay too long
for being stuck in a dark place such as my mind
will leave you feeling quite insane

CHAPTER ONE: THE CAUSE

Mental illness can affect anyone. Contrary to popular belief, there isn't always a cause of mental illness. Yes, I was bullied as a child, and I'm sure that bullying played a part in how I grew up. I was bullied every year in elementary school, mostly for my looks. To those bullies, I have this to say: Thank you. Yes, you made me feel ugly and hate myself, but if it weren't for you, I wouldn't be as strong as I am today. I wouldn't be able to battle with myself as well as I have, so thank you. Yes, I had a physical disability due to being born premature, but other than those two things, my life was pretty normal. I had friends. I did my school work, and I did it well.

My worst enemy is myself. I have always put impossible expectations on myself. It wasn't my parents who were strict and who wanted me to get at least 80's in school, it was me. I would call myself names and beat myself up if I didn't achieve a goal that I had set for myself. I usually set myself up for failure, as I made the goals impossible to reach, yet I made myself tired and worn out by jumping with all of my might to get to them, and always falling short.

From a young age, I learned to despise myself. I learned that whatever I did was never good enough. I learned that good marks in school were expected. I learned to strive for perfection and nothing less. For all of these things, I had myself to blame.

My Enemy (Written 2010)
There's this person.
This person thinks too much and when I mess up,
this person is the first to tear me down.
I hate this person, but at the same time, I can never get rid of them
because this person,
is me.

CHAPTER TWO: ANXIETY

I've always been an anxious kid, I can't think of a time in my life when I wasn't worried about the future, about what I'm going to say, what I'm doing. It got to the point where anxiety was controlling my life. I wouldn't go to social gatherings because I might say something stupid, I wouldn't ask any questions for the fear of being told "no". I was that quiet, shy, invisible girl at school; always doing her work, always getting good marks, always being ignored. My mind was constantly racing, looking for something, anything, to worry about.

I would make lists of my worries, just to make them stop racing around my head. There wasn't a single moment of the day where I wasn't worrying. I was also a perfectionist. Sounds good right? Always get good marks, always pushing yourself to do well, so you never slack off, sounds great! Trust me when I say that it definitely isn't great. Sure, you get great marks, but at what cost? The cost of always pressuring yourself to do well, never letting yourself "let things go". I had to be perfect, or else I would get so mad at myself; I would scream at my reflection in the mirror and pull my hair out. Doesn't sound so great anymore, does it? Your whole life revolves around the need to be perfect.

Worries (Written 2011)
I worry...
that my friends will leave me
that my family doesn't love me
that I'm ugly
that I'm stupid
that I'll fail
that people will be mad at me
that I'm wrong
that I worry too much
that I won't make it
that these worries will never go away

CHAPTER THREE: DEPRESSION

I can't pinpoint exactly when the depression started. I've always known that the winter months were particularly hard, with the grey skies and gloomy days, but once summer showed itself with sun rays and no school, I would be less stressed and much happier. This was the typical routine for about three years, until one summer when instead of leaving me, the sadness just deepened. Instead of spending time with friends and tanning in the sun, I was stuck in bed, unable to move. It is too easy to be perceived as laziness when in fact the mere thought of movement physically hurts. Your limbs are aching as you lay in bed, watching the sunlight shine through your window, and you cry because you have no idea what is happening to you.

I don't remember much of that summer, just constantly crying and not knowing why, feeling as if whatever I did wasn't good enough, wishing I could just go outside and enjoy the weather instead of being stuck inside. When you have depression, you don't always realize that you're isolating yourself. It just happens. One text to a friend that you're cancelling plans once again, another day you spend alone in your room, another week where you don't shower. You don't realize it, but you're pushing everyone away, you're making yourself become completely and utterly alone.

I remember feeling so fragile and broken, just waiting for something to push me so that I broke down. It's odd, how one day, you're used to crying every day about nothing and feeling deeply and profoundly sad, and the next you feel so empty and numb. You want the tears to fall, but they don't.

Sadness (Written June 19th, 2013)

Infinite sadness swells up inside,

it looms over me like a threat

it gathers itself within me, it's doors not opening yet

it shows itself in the blank-eyed stares;

the silent tear rolling down my cheek

it shows itself in the way that I carry myself,

like a faucet that has a leak

it's sister emotions are empty and lonely

together they move as one

to wreck havoc inside of my brain and tell my bony legs to run

the emptiness is so vast and the loneliness is like a black hole

together paired with sadness they will destroy me

and achieve their goal

CHAPTER 4: INSOMNIA

Sleeping becomes an escape from every day life. You either sleep too much or too little. Originally, my worries and anxious thoughts racing around my mind kept me up all night and left me exhausted with bags under my eyes. Once depression settled in, I couldn't get enough sleep. Everything was okay for the few hours that I slept. It was a blissful and welcome distraction from my mind.

Insomnia (Written June 5th, 2013)

sleep, once my favourite escape,

is now a constant headache

I stare at the clock watching time pass me by

with my head on the pillow covered in tears that are now dry

my mind is either busy as a bee

or is lost as if out at sea

this feeling of numbness I have inside

stays with me all throughout the night

as I look to the sky and see the sun rise

I look at my reflection and notice my eyes

the bags under my eyes hold my hopes and dreams

I smile on the outside while my mind screams

CHAPTER 5: SELF HARM

I once promised my friends and family that I would never self-harm. I broke this promise like many others that I had made. Self-harm is an unhealthy coping mechanism. Some self-harm for an escape, to feel something other than numbness, because they feel they deserve it, and because it becomes something comforting and something that they are familiar with. I self-harmed for all of these reasons.

Beginning to self-harm was the worst decision I have ever made. Please, if you are thinking of starting, don't. I know what you might be thinking, "I will never lose control, I won't become addicted, it's only one little cut." I've been there, I've thought those same things, and I was very wrong. It started out as something to do when I was stressed or extremely angry at myself, and then progressed to once or twice a month, to once a week, to at least once a day. I realized that I was no longer in control; I was addicted and I needed help.

Bracelet (Written October 10th, 2011)

she wears a bracelet of scars

delicately stitched around her wrist

she wears a fake smile

that fools everyone

her eyes still shine

yet she has lost her light

her emotions are like waves in the sea

sometimes calm

sometimes a tsunami

at the end of the day she collapses

as the waves crash over her

and she sinks into her sadness

CHAPTER 6: GETTING HELP

Realizing that you need help is a very hard thing to come to terms with. When I first started seeing my guidance counsellor at my high school, I thought that I was just under a lot of stress and needed to just talk it out. After many sessions with her, she recommended seeing a professional for my anxiety, since it was controlling my life. I was often having panic attacks over (what I thought) were silly things such as the thought of my friends leaving me, the future, and school projects.

For those of you who don't know what a panic attack is, let me explain. In my experience, panic attacks are when you're gasping for air, your chest hurts, your negative thoughts are attacking you and you have no control over them. All you can do is sit there crying your eyes out, and wait for it to pass. You feel as if you're losing your mind and you have a wicked headache. Luckily for me, I haven't passed out from these panic attacks.

I couldn't have asked for a better guidance counsellor; she was always there to listen and offer sound advice. It got to a point where I spent more time in her office than I did in actual classes, which is when we realized that I should get help outside of school. The wait list to see a psychiatrist was eight months long. That is such a long waiting time, especially since once kids are able to ask for help, it usually means that they have dealt with their illnesses for quite some time now, and are at a loss at how to go forward.

This transition into getting professional help happened for me during my senior year of high school. In my grade twelve year, I was rarely at school due to the fact that it physically hurt me to get out of bed, I was procrastinating my school work as I barely had the energy to get myself into the shower. There would be weeks where I would wear the same thing to school. I started to not care how others saw me, as every day became a vicious routine. On the days where I could, I would wake up, drag myself out of bed, go to school, come home, go back to bed and repeat. I pushed everyone away, rarely talking, just surviving the day. I always felt alone, exhausted, numb, and invisible.

It was around the end of March of 2013 when, as per request of my therapist, I went to the local general hospital and signed myself into the adolescent crisis centre. I didn't just walk right into the centre, no, I had to wait six hours in the Emergency waiting room before being seen by a social worker and then a psychiatrist who assessed me. I ended up being put into the crisis unit that night. I was there for only five days before being transferred to a long-term mental health facility.

It wasn't until I arrived at the facility and was settled into my room that it really hit me; if I'm in here, that means that I really am sick. I'm not just making it all up. Until this moment, I had shrugged it all off as me making it up, there's no way that I actually need help! The truth hit me like a ton of bricks, I am sick and am in a mental hospital.

The next four months would be a journey filled with love, hurt, pain, death, life, and eventually, recovery and hope. I learned to like living in the hospital. The friends I made in there understood me. The nurses were nice and always available to talk and help. The food actually wasn't as bad as you might think.

Being in hospital shelters you from the real world; no cell phones and no internet. I found peace in that and realized who my true friends were: those who made an effort to contact me or who actually wanted to be present in my life. It was hard to think of the fact that while my friends and classmates were planning their prom and signing yearbooks, I was in a hospital taking medications and going to group therapy. I made some really good friends in the adolescent unit, because they understood what I was going through and they had battled the illnesses like I had.

Getting better doesn't happen overnight. Trust me, I wish it did! The most crucial component to starting your path to recovery is that you have to want it. Doctors can give you medication, therapists can give you coping strategies and all of the talk therapy in the world; but if you don't want to get better, you won't. That's one of the hardest things to do when you're battling depression is to get better because the depression would much rather stay rooted in your system for the rest of your life. You're literally fighting with yourself. As soon as you have just the tiniest sense of wanting to get better, you start to see changes.

Personally, it took me four months before a tiny part of me wanted to get better. There were many days where I was perfectly content with just giving up, giving in to the illness. Many days were spent crying, fighting myself, and not knowing who I was or what I had turned into. As soon as I found that I wanted to get better, even just a little bit, I latched onto that hope and hung onto it for dear life.

I'm not saying that once you want to be better you will magically recover and be your old self without the mental illness, no not at all. You're going to have to fight even harder to give that tiny bit of hope a chance to grow. It will be exhausting, there will be days where you want to give up, but as long as you keep that tiny piece of hope with you, you will recover.

CHAPTER 7: A PRISONER OF MY OWN MIND

The following are poems that I wrote while as an inpatient at the mental health facility. *Warning: they may be triggering to some people, please read with caution and if you are struggling with mental illness, don't be ashamed to ask for help.*

Numb (written April 5th, 2013)

today I am numb

the wind blows in between my ribcage

words whirl by without being heard

although I am sad, tears do not fall from my dry eyes

I glance around the room, seeing nothing

~

Cold (Written April 18th, 2013)

coldness seeps through my bones

straight to my heart

making me numb

am I really here?

am I a real person?

the feeling of sadness creeps back in

taking residence within me once again

hello, old friend

~

Sack of Bones (Written May 5th, 2013)

I am numb

I feel pain radiating from my wrist

like it was set on fire

I have dry eyes

and no words to offer

to anyone around me

I am a sack of bones that creates a person

I am nothing

the only sound is my automatic breathing

while my feeble heart

fights to keep me alive

~

Stuck (Written May 18th, 2013)

I'm stuck in a depressive state

everything around me is so dark

I can't remember what I last ate

I want to move forward but I'm stuck in park

I can't see a way out of this place

I slash signs on my wrist that I can't follow

all of my thoughts run around in a race

where my heart should be it is empty and hollow

I only have one dream, one thrill,

it's very sad but oh so real

I need to swallow these pills

in order to make the ultimate deal

I look outside and see miserable rain

my eyes slowly close and I see a light

if I'm lucky, it might be a train

maybe this time I'll finally do something right

~

Dandelions (Written May 18th, 2013)

dandelions show up in the grass

inserting themselves where they aren't wanted

dandelions are very hard to ignore

and could be confused with a flower

my negative thoughts are dandelions

inserting themselves in my mind

I can't ignore these thoughts and at times

believe that they are the truth

~

Aches (Written June 4th, 2013)

head aches

heart aches

body aches

mind aches

life is full of pain and mistakes

empty promises and enough tears to create a river

sad teens with smiling faces gather all around

they fill their pockets with their feelings, heavy as can be,

they make their way to the lake which is full of empty hopes and broken down dreams

one by one they jump into the water

slowly sinking towards the bottom, a peaceful look upon their face

their feelings finally became useful, anchoring them to the ground

darkness slowly enfolds them as death knocks on their doors

taking all of the secrets that they don't need to keep anymore

~

Demons (Written June 10th, 2013)

they were wrong but oh so right

I am the girl, the one who lost her fight

I fight with different demons, they reside within my soul

they make me strive for perfection, to fit into impossible roles

the demons, they are laughing

calling my pathetic life a joke

they make me want to do odd things

like wear a necklace made of rope

these demons, my companions, they wait for that one night

to unleash themselves upon the world and make everything right

to you, the readers of this poem, I say to you goodbye

I warn you to be careful because the demons are out tonight

and will not rest until the moment that I die

~

Thin (Written June 11th, 2013)

I look into the mirror and don't like what I see

the person that hates me the most is staring right back at me

people tend to use me and walk over me like a mat

they also think I'm skinny when all I see is fat

I need to lose weight, to make those numbers lower

it's a way of committing suicide, but just a little slower

the calories add up inside me, making me a balloon

I eat, and eat, and eat until I'm the size of the moon

with a finger down my throat I watch my problems flush away

or maybe I'll get skinny by eating one less meal a day

I look into the mirror and don't like what I see

this is my little secret and I'm throwing out the key

~

Rock Bottom (Written June 13th, 2013)

to hang there with a rope necklace is all that I desire

wait, hold on, I'm doing fine; just call me a liar

to take that last step, and dangle in the air

all of my feelings and thoughts are too much to bear

oh how I long to not walk this earth anymore

the certainty of death radiates down into my core

I am nothing but an empty shell, the girl inside is no longer there

to tell you the truth, I'm not doing too well

I'm trying so hard not to care

I know that I'll hurt my family and friends

it hurts me deep inside

but the near perfect solution is that this must end, Jennifer has already died

I am no longer with you, I am merely numb and empty

do not miss me too much, but please,

live on without me

~

Alone (Written June 13th, 2013)

I'm alone with my sadness

my only companion is my suicidal thoughts

everything is a black hole, especially my mind

I want to destroy myself

I have lost my will to live, it has run off with my hope

leaving me miserable and lonely

outside, the weather strongly contrasts with me

as many times as the sun and clouds come out, the faster I sink into the dark abyss

the darkness surrounds me, comforting,

as it is the feeling that I have grown to accept and feel the most

it seems friendly at first, makes you sleepy,

keeps you company when you push everyone else away

but then, it attacks

it now controls you, taking a hold on your thoughts and turning them against you

with a dizzying spiral of shame and self-hatred

it makes you despise the monster you've become

you see the only way to rid yourself of the darkness is to make everything quiet forever

you no longer want to live, and that scares you

~

Filth (Written June 20th, 2013)

water and blood

mixing together to form a trail of red

it drips slowly down my arm and takes the worries from my head

as I wash my hair and body with soap, I cut my arm as a way to cope

A slight sting on my arm as it comes in contact with the water

with all of these scars I have on my right,

is this what you would call a good daughter?

drying off after my shower I look down at my arm

I look at the lines etched into my skin

another day that I have self-harmed

~

Party (Written June 20th 2013)

my kind of cocktail is of the pill variety

my slice of heaven is a slice on my wrist

my idea of a fancy necklace is a rope

I get drunk off of self-hatred and loneliness

the easiest thing to do is sleep, it's better than being awake

the hardest thing to do is stay alive, depression would much rather have the other way

it's a terrible battle but I'm determined to win

even if it kills me to try, at least I tried

to escape from the monster

~

Escape (Written June 21st, 2013)

the place that I'm in is worse than hell

it seems that I'm a prisoner, although I cannot tell

I want a one-way ticket out of here

this place, it knows all of my deepest fears

I need to escape or I will be dead

can you please get me out of here?

out of my head?

~

Sleep (Written June 21st 2013)

sleep: my best friend and my enemy

it comforts me or leaves me feeling lonely

dreams of a better life or nightmares of disaster

it lets me leave my life for a few hours

but leaves me for a harsh wake up call in the morning

I can press snooze and get comfy or get up and grudgingly face the day

I can have too much or not enough

sleep: my best friend and my enemy

~

Light (Written June 23rd 2013)

I open my eyes and realize that there's a tiny light

it shimmers through the darkness and resides to my right

how did I not notice that it was there before?

how did I not see this heavy little door?

upon closer inspection it's only open a bit

I try to open it and although it doesn't budge, I don't quit

after hours of trying, I am tired and spent

looking at that light, I notice that it's a bit bigger

I have made a dent

I lay back and close my eyes

knowing that I'm making progress and getting somewhere

I'm not exactly sure where that is and that's okay

I'll let you know when I get there

~

Pride (Written June 24th 2013)

there's a feeling inside me that I do not know

this alien feeling is a good one though

pride swells up as I realize the accomplishments I've done

although they seem like small, ordinary things,

when battling a mental illness it's a war that I've won

while in a mental hospital I've successfully finished high school

I now look forward to lazy summer days of swimming in my pool

it's funny how last week I wanted to be dead

now, I have a life to look forward to instead

~

Darkness (Written June 30th 2013)

as the sun sets and darkness fills the sky

the light in my brain goes out, I don't know why

my brain works fast

making me overdose on thoughts

my hot tears fall from my face and onto the page making tiny dots

I feel as if my friends are leaving me

I feel lost and alone

I'm wandering around

trying to find a place to call my home

~

Home (Written July 8th 2013)

Tomorrow's the day I pack my bags and go home
I'm learning that this doesn't mean that I'll never feel alone
Being discharged doesn't mean that I'm cured
I'm still searching for something
I still need to be heard

There is still darkness in my brain
but some new knowledge as well
so next time I have a depressive episode
it won't be like this hell

I am ready to face the world
armed with coping strategies and assertiveness
death
despair and
suicide are tenants of my brain that I will surely not miss

If they try to sneak back in and reclaim their homes I know exactly what to do
I'll take out my strategies and tools and I'll defeat them
which will be very new

The battle is not yet over
in fact
it has just begun

It will leave me bruised and tired
but this time

it will be <u>me</u> who has won

~

Recovery (Written July 9th, 2013)

recovery is a tricky process
two steps forward, one step back
your mind is constantly waiting for another unwelcome attack
you will never be 100% better, I fear that is the unfortunate truth
but this time you control the depression instead of it controlling you
each day that you're recovering is a day that you have won
trust me, I know that living with a mental illness is never easy and fun

there will be times of relapse, feelings of guilt and pain
it is all a part of recovery, you don't need to be ashamed
the journey through recovery is hard and has twisted and winding roads
but when it comes to choosing a road, you will know exactly which way to go

you owe it to yourself to recover and see the light
to get past the darkness and pain and see the sun shining bright
you deserve to be happy, loved, and kind
not only to others but to yourself
and be at ease in your mind

~

CHAPTER 8: INSIGHT

When I was in the hospital, many of the doctors and nurses would tell me that I am one of the most insightful patients that they've had. It's true, I am insightful, but that doesn't mean that I can easily fix my problems.

If asked, I could tell you everything that is wrong with me. I could point out the defence mechanisms I am using, I can tell you that a thought that I am having is irrational and that I need to change it. What I can't do, however, is do exactly that; change it.

I know that most of my fears are irrational, but that doesn't make them any less scary or real in my mind. I know that I worry too much and am very hard on myself, but I can't stop doing either or those things. I am insightful, but can't apply changes to myself.

It's similar to taking your own advice, you simply can't. If a friend were in the exact same situation you're in, you could easily tell them what they should do to make themselves happy. Now, put yourself in that situation and you're at a loss of what to do.

CHAPTER 9: RELAPSE

There will be days where you want to throw in the towel and forget all of your hard work and succumb to the illness. On those days, it's okay if the only thing you accomplished was staying alive. On those days, it's okay to cry and not be okay, as long as you get back up. On those days, don't give up.

I'd be lying if I said that once I got discharged I never thought of suicide or self harming. I'd be lying if I said that I'll never get sad ever again.

The truth is, you will have days where you're sad and you don't know why. You will have days where all you can think about is suicide. You will have days where you want to, or may even, self harm. You will have days that completely and utterly suck. I just want you to know that you shouldn't be ashamed if you relapse, because you are still working towards recovery. Recovery is not a smooth path, it's a very bumpy one that has many setbacks and obstacles. Relapse is bound to happen, this does not mean that you have failed. This does not mean that you're never going to get better. This does not mean that you have returned to your old habits for good. It means that you are a warrior. It means that you are fighting. It means that you have been knocked down, but you can and will get back up. It means that you're getting stronger. It means that you are going through the recovery process, and I am proud of you.

CHAPTER 10: LIFE ON THE OUTSIDE

Once I was discharged from the hospital, life didn't resume as it was before my major depressive episode. In fact, it was much different. Life on the outside is very different than being a patient at a hospital. In the hospital, you are sheltered from your regular life. You can refuse to take phone calls and not have to deal with every day drama. Once you're discharged, it feels as if you are left completely alone as everything from your every day life overwhelms you.

There will be a period of time where you get inexplicably low, and feel as you did before being admitted to the hospital. Please know that this is normal.

CHAPTER 11: POEMS ON THE OUTSIDE

You Left (Written January 24th, 2014)
You said,
'People tend to tell you that they're there for you,
but don't live up to it. I promise that I'll live up to it."

I knew,
that wasn't the case but I hoped,
that I was wrong and you would be there for me,
as promised.

I pushed everyone away, isolating myself as the
depression whispered temptations in my ears.
You said, "You clearly want space. I'll leave you alone."

Inside, I was screaming: no, come back.
Outside, I was silent.

You said,
"I'd never leave you, no matter what."

I'm sitting here, saying nothing
while you're doing what you promised you would never do.

You left,
and never looked back.
~

Trying To Make Sense Of Things (Written July 21st, 2014)
I have feelings.
Feelings that most people around me do not understand.
They don't understand what a struggle it is to get out of bed in the morning,
thinking that life seems pretty okay when you're asleep.
They don't understand how something so simple can make me overwhelmed.
Falling face first into a pit of panic and unknown.
They don't understand feeling as if your emotions are a glass floor and anything, at any
given moment can make it break and leave you falling into a world of darkness.
I have feelings that even I do not understand.

Do you know how many times the thoughts go through my head,
that maybe it would be better if I slept forever?
Of course you don't, you wouldn't.
I know that sleeping forever is not the most logical answer,
nor is it going to help anything.
I know that I'm stronger than this thing

~

Self Harm (Written November 22nd, 2014)

my smile slips away
as the metal connects with skin
dancing that familiar dance,
creating new patterns.

I deserve these red tears that my skin sheds.
I deserve the names I call myself,
the hate I feel inside me that is a black hole.

I tug and pull and am finally able
to put that smile back on
which gets harder to do every time.

I step outside and mutter the words that will
comfort you,
"I'm fine."

~

It Doesn't Matter (Written January 25th, 2014)

It doesn't matter
how many songs I listen to
how much I have to drink
how many cigarettes I smoke
hoe many tears I shed
how many cuts I have;
none of it will bring you back.

~

Leaves (Written February 20th, 2014)

I wish it were easy
to put my thoughts onto paper
but my mind is an empty void filled with
thoughts that are more scattered than
autumn leaves falling
haphazardly on the ground.

Vacation (Written February 25th, 2014)

people on vacation are happy
I am still sad
self-conscious of my belly
and the scars that I have.
the sky is blue and the wind is warm but
to me everything is grey.
I am a brewing storm,
the sea is calm and this is a lovely boat
dark thoughts crash over me
in waves and I'm continuously
losing hope.

~

Winter Wind (Written March 16th, 2014)

the winter wind chills me to my core
I can't feel joy anymore.
all I feel is sadness and anger
suicidal thoughts put my life in danger
I am empty
I am nothing
I am so completely tired of fighting.

~

What I Know (Written April 11h, 2014)

a cheery hospital name
but the patients are not so,
mood disorders and medication
are all that I know

hospital food can be quite bland
the activities not much fun
I am here because I had decided that my life was done

another year, another age,
yet I'm still at this place
of chemical imbalance and
unstable mental states.

I don't know how long I'll be here
how long I'll be sick inside;
until I'm feeling better
and no longer wish to die.

You're Not Alone, I Have It Too (Written April 12th, 2014)

you're not alone, I have it too
mental illness is not something that you choose
it doesn't matter if you're rich or poor
smart or dumb
if you have 100 friends or simply one.

it is a sickness such as cancer or the flu
it is something that doesn't have to control you.

it may feel like your fault but
I can assure you that it's not
the cure for this is not easily bought.
it takes time and effort to recover from this
but once you do, it's not something you'll miss.

surround yourself with people who
love and support you and remember
you're not alone, because I have it too.

~

5 AM Poem (Written April 19th, 2014)

I can love 20 people and still want to die
they'll say "but you are loved" or
"people love you" but it all sounds like lies.
sometimes love isn't enough
and your head is full of so much stuff
and all you want to do is die.
there are some things that I would like to say to you:
one - you are incredibly brave
two - keep fighting, I know that it's hard but
you are a warrior who can provide the comfort you crave
three - it will take time and it will take effort
but you can and will win
four - you are a strong person
I know you believe it's not true but just take my
word for it and keep surviving and fighting
and most importantly being kind to you.

~

Anxieties (Written April 22nd, 2014)

I fear the unknown and I hate when
plans suddenly change.

*in a crowded room I always feel alone
and am terrified of being on stage.
feeling the heat of everyone's stares
I always feel like I'm being judged
I hate social situations and
in everyone's eyes I see glares.
anxieties are flooding my brain
depression is weighing me down
I feel as if I'm completely insane
the dress I've worn most is a hospital gown.*

~

I Am A Ghost (Written May 2nd, 2014)

*the girl you seek is no longer here
I don't know who has replaced her but
she is sad and sheds quite a few tears.
she rarely smiles and wishes to die
she is not the sweet darling
"Jennifer" as you know her by.
stop visiting, stop calling
the one who answers is not who you want
this girl is empty, simply a shell
this "Jennifer" is merely a ghost who is very unwell
this girl is not a person
this girl is not real
yet gets overwhelmed by the emotions she feels
I am not what you expect
I am not who you think
I am dead inside
already a ghost who communicates
via spilled ink*

~

Thunderstorms (Written May 13th, 2014)

I find comfort in thunderstorms

*maybe it's the way that the sky opens up and cries
the way I often do at night*

*maybe it's the way that lighting flashes
strong and fast
like the anger I feel inside*

*maybe it's the way that thunder rumbles
like a constant shout,*

"hear me! I am here and alive"

or maybe it's simply the way that
there is beauty in a storm
~

Tears Will Not Fall (Written May 18th, 2014)
it's an odd feeling
being so sad but unable to cry
all I can do is stare at the clock
and watch the hours pass by
it's as if I'm numb
the feeling of emptiness seeps down to my core
am I even a real person?
can I cope with this anymore?
I wish that it would rain and
the drops would remind my eyes
that they can rain too
but the sun is glaring at me through the window
not a raindrop in sight
I feel the dryness of my cheeks and realize I'm right
tears will not fall from my eyes
~

Weight (Written May 24th, 2014)
the weight is dropping
I have a huge smile on my face
while everyone looks on with a hint of distaste

skipping meals is not a good way to lose weight
because once you start it's hard to stop

it's too bad that the only real smile
I've had this past month was seeing the number drop
~

Stuck (Written June 14th, 2014)
I'm stuck in this hole
I see no way out
It's so dark in here
I've got no voice to shout

I'm hitting brick walls
one's that are stuck in my brain

this is so frustrating
I'm going insane

medicine doesn't help
I'm severely depressed
will this dark cloud lift?
will I be put at rest?

summer is here
the weather is hot
I'm still hopeless
but fighting with
what little energy I've got

~

Self Injury (Written June 19th, 2014)
the urge to self harm is strong
it's my very own coping strategy
but I know that it's wrong

there's got to be a better way
to show what I'm feeling
I look at my arms
and see my scars healing

this addiction has control over me
hell bent on self destruction
is not a good place to be

I want the outside to reflect my inner pain
so I harm myself to make me feel sane

~

Tiny Prick Of Light (Written June 25th, 2014)
there's this tiny prick of light within my realm of darkness
if you look too hard or scan quickly you won't see it
it isn't there all of the time
in fact it made it's first appearance today
it flickers on and off like a star saying goodnight
if I look for that light now I don't see it
it's almost a trick of the eye, this tiny light of hope
I think it's important that I'm seeing it at all
no matter how bright or how frequent
sometimes a tiny prick of light is all I need
to latch onto and never let go

sometimes it means that I do have a future
sometimes it means I should stay alive for another day
and sometimes it means nothing at all

~

I Am Just A Girl (Written July 8th, 2014)
I'm just a girl with messy hair and glass eyes
I'm just a girl who is empty inside
I'm just a girl whose words on paper make more sense
than the words that are inside of her head
I'm just a girl who is spending time on a psych ward
I'm just a girl who doesn't care about life anymore
I'm just a girl who has lost control
I'm just a girl who doesn't know where to go
I'm just a girl who doesn't know what to decide
I'm just a girl who doesn't recognize her own mind
I'm just a girl who writes poems to express
the only feelings she has are
anger, sadness, and emptiness

~

Thank You For Being Alive (Written July 11th, 2014)
I'm glad that you're alive
I know it's dark but one day you'll shine

I know how it feels to want to give up
to feel so depressed that your life feels stuck
to feel frozen in place as the world moves around you
and stay in bed because it's all you can do
to feel so out of control
as if your emotions are a speeding car
that you don't know how to drive
but remember this:
I'm glad you're alive

~

Empty (Written July 16th, 2014)
I am empty
I am numb
nothing I do is any fun
my mind is blank and
I have depression to thank for
making my life miserable and sad
if I feel anything I feel mad

for being sick
for being here
sitting in a hospital for another year
even if I wanted to cry, I can't
I just stare blankly at the wall
while my cheeks stay dry
I feel as if I'm just wasting time
I am a prisoner of my own mind
~

I'm Scared (Written August 29th, 2014)
getting better can be scary
although I know it's very necissary

it's standing on the edge of a cliff
one foot raised
it's stepping into the unknown
which makes me so afraid

I'm comforted by my sadness
it is all that I know
but in order to recover
I have to let it go
~

New Lessons (Written October 21st, 2014)
they teach you that i comes before e except after c
but they don't teach you how to look in the mirror
and appreciate what you see
they teach you that 2 plus 2 equals 4
but they don't teach you how to not hate yourself down to the core
they teach you to shout when you're angry
but they don't teach you how to love yourself
they teach you how to grow up intelligent
but emotionally unstable
they teach you history and how to give others labels

we need to be taught to care about others
we need to be taught how to love outselves
and put ourselves first
we need to be taught that it's okay to not be okay
we need to be taught that we aren't alone
we need to be taught new lessons
~

What Depression Is To Me (Written December 9th, 2014)
depression is like watching everyone around you
live their lives while you're frozen in place
depression is a constant black cloud
that only you can see
depression is an old fur coat
providing comfort and a sense of safety
depression is lacking enough energy
to complete simple tasks
it's not showering
aching muscles
blank stares
and "I don't know" to questions asked
depression is long days and nights
unable to get out of bed
it's a mental illness
one I have inside my head
remember, having depression does not
make you flawed or weak
it is a chemical imbalance in the brain
getting help can be scary
but can provide the relief that you seek

~

ECT (Written October 16th, 2015)
my vision is fading as the anaesthetic is racing through veins
as blue as an empty ocean filled with flesh eating sharks.
my brain is zapped in hopes to prevent an
oncoming mental illness attack.
I'm dazed and confused as I look around the room
I should be happy to be awake and to have a heart beating too.
I'm sad and alone and I wish I was skin and bones
but instead I will eat or maybe put up my feet
as electric currents travel my brain.

~

CHAPTER 12: THE END

To You, the reader,

Thank you for reading this book of mine. I hope you enjoyed a little glimpse inside of my mind. If you relate to anything that I have shared in this book, I encourage you to seek help. Yes, it's scary and you might not want to accept the fact that you need it, but it helps you in the long run. There is always help available, don't be afraid to ask for it. Please do not think that your problems are not as important as someone else's, because you matter, and your life matters. Remember that sometimes it's okay to not be okay, and to be kind to yourself. Stay strong, you are a fighter.

Kids Help Phone: 1-800-668-6868
Suicide Hotline: www.suicidehotlines.com
Canadian Mental Health Association: www.cmha.ca
If you, or someone you know needs immediate help, call 9-1-1